NATIONAL GEOGRAPHIC

School Publishing

D0503506

THE ENERGY OF Water

PIONEER EDITION

By Barbara Keeler

CONTENTS

Water Power. Water energy makes electricity for millions of people.

THE ENERGY OF
Water

Water crashes! It goes over the waterfall. It rushes downriver. This is Niagara Falls. Many people visit it each year. But it's more than a vacation spot. The Niagara River leads into the falls. It is a source of energy. The fast-moving water has lots of energy. Let's learn how this energy has been used over the years.

By Barbara Keeler

Waterwheels

For thousands of years, people used the energy from flowing water. They used it to help them do work. Waterwheels help use water's energy. A waterwheel is a wheel turned by water. It has paddles or cups around its edge. Moving water flows against the paddles or cups. The moving water turns the wheel. When the wheel turns, it creates energy.

People use this energy to do work. Waterwheels were often used to grind corn or grain. They were also used to cut wood. They were used to spin cotton and do many other things.

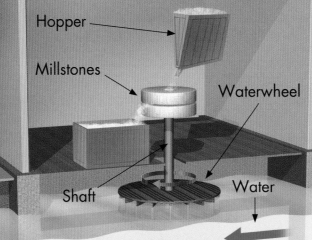

Working Wheel. This shows an early waterwheel in a mill. The waterwheel turned a millstone. Millstones were used to grind grain.

Big Wheel. This waterwheel is in Syria. It is thousands of years old. It still works today.

The World Changes

Water power and waterwheels helped change the way people worked.

Richard Arkwright invented a **machine**. It made strong yarn. Yarn is cotton thread. It looks like string. It is used to weave cloth. Arkwright used energy from waterwheels to run his machines. The waterwheel passed its energy to the machine.

People began to put many machines in one building. That's called a factory. This helped them do more work.

More Power. Millraces give more power to waterwheels. They flow more water to a waterwheel.

People's Lives Changed

Using moving water for energy changed people's lives. In the early 1800s cotton cloth-making machines came to the United States. The machines used waterwheels for power. Soon there were many cloth-making mills in New England.

The new mills and factories changed the way people lived. People moved away from farms. They came to mill towns. There they could work in factories. Soon more people had factory jobs than farm jobs.

Electricity from Water

Waterwheels aren't used much today. But we still use moving water for energy. What type of energy? Electricity! How? Water flows through a power plant. This is called a **hydroelectric plant**. A hydroelectric plant changes the energy from moving water to electrical energy.

Moving water flows through the plant. It pushes blades in a **turbine**. The turbine spins. It acts like a waterwheel. The turbine turns a structure in a **generator**. The generator makes electricity.

Flooded with Power. Hydroelectric plants are often built in dams.

Creating Energy. Turbines look like waterwheels lying on their sides.

Motion of the Ocean

Oceans are the biggest bodies of water. Just think how much energy is in them. Have you ever seen a huge ocean wave? It rises and falls. All that energy can become electricity.

Several inventions use ocean energy. Some machines sit on the ocean floor. They capture water energy as water flows past. Other machines bob up and down on waves. The motion makes electricity.

The first wave farm opened in 2008. It produces ocean energy. There may be more wave farms in the future.

The Past and the Future

People have come a long way using the energy of moving water. Long ago they used it to grind grain. Now we use it to make electricity. Who knows how we'll use it next!

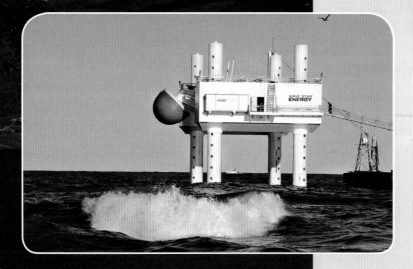

Riding the Wave. This machine is lowered down to the waves. It uses their power.

WORDWISE

generator: an invention that changes energy of motion into electrical energy

hydroelectric plant: place where moving water is used to generate electricity

machine: something that makes work easier

turbine: a wheel that turns a structure inside a generator

FUEL FROM Water

Did you know there's fuel in water? Water has hydrogen in it. Hydrogen can be used for fuel. The energy in hydrogen can run cars. It can run other vehicles, too. It can even run the space shuttle!

Making Hydrogen

Hydrogen is usually not found by itself. It's in other matter. Hydrogen is in plants. It's also in the ground. But it costs a lot to separate it from other matter. And it uses a lot of energy. So scientists are looking for better ways to get hydrogen.

Today, some cars run on hydrogen. Why? A hydrogen car does not make pollution. The only thing it gives off is water. So using hydrogen is good for the environment. Maybe someday you'll drive a hydrogen car!

Fueling Up. This station provides hydrogen for hydrogen cars.

Hydrogen

Green Energy. This machine contains algae. It's a living thing. It's like a plant. Scientists are testing it. They think it may produce hydrogen for cars and other machines.

Water Energy

Go with the flow to answer these questions about water power.

1 What makes a waterwheel turn?

2 What types of work did waterwheels do for people?

3 How did the energy of water change how people worked?

4 How is water used to make electricity?

5 Why is hydrogen better for the environment than liquid fuel?